UNLOCKING CREATIVITY

UNLOCKING CREATIVITY

Techniques for Inspired Living

B. VINCENT

QuantumQuill Press

CONTENTS

1 Introduction 1
2 Understanding Creativity 3
3 Techniques for Unlocking Creativity 5
4 Applying Creativity in Daily Life 11

Copyright © 2024 by B. Vincent

All rights reserved. No part of this book may be reproduced in any manner whatsoever without written permission except in the case of brief quotations embodied in critical articles and reviews.

First Printing, 2024

CHAPTER 1

Introduction

Everything that has made life bearable, meaningful, enjoyable, and beautiful for us is a product of the talents and creativity of someone like the architect of a building, the mathematician who discovered the rules that are the foundation of the internet, the clothing designer, the hairstylist, the chef, etc. The work of all these people demonstrates the breadth of the concept of creativity. Each of us has this creativity within us, and it just needs us to unlock our potential.

Two of the most common myths are that only some people are creative and that creativity is the sole domain of the arts. The truth is that we are all creative; we just need to awaken our individual potential and develop it. Similarly, while it is true that the classical music composer, the actor with talents, the inspiring poet, the painter of genius, and the ingenious writer have made a remarkable contribution to society, this does not mean that these are the only forms of creativity.

When creativity is unlocked, there is an increase in harmony within the universe and a sense of cooperation comes into play, instead of the selfish needs of the different parts of creation. Therefore, it is important to take time assessing our creativity and finding ways of growing it. There are various techniques that we can utilize in order for us to live an inspired life.

CHAPTER 2

Understanding Creativity

Because the phenomena involved in the quality of a state of mind or of great works of art appertain only to distant aspects of this understanding, or else stand outside the compass of ordinary discussion, a miscomprehension has grown up around 'creativity'. Far from being a special quality set aside for the pathologically inclined, common sense indicates that the admired attribute must necessarily reside in all, just as, we commonly grant, humor or instants of moral action transcend our limitations to fill all with their shining quality. Yet, the gross incomprehension in this delicate matter never implements a bridge over both fact and communication of different and sometimes opposing aspects of 'morality' or 'evolution'.

The creative act involves an artificial division between the 'outer' and 'inner'. It is often mistakenly assumed that the world and self are independent entities: if we are concerned with 'the moment', the self is thought of as wholly outside it, and the moment in which the creator of art and the work of art become one is no more perceived than is the fact that a poet's verses are totally unconnected with his inmost feelings. The mystery surrounding the inexplicable relationship leads some to deny that they have any 'creations' at all. It leads many more to see anything they create as an expression of their secret self, and others to recognize that however unconnected with their moments, their works are an inner and unspoken chronicle of their lives.

CHAPTER 3

Techniques for Unlocking Creativity

Many people are blocked by the words used by professionals when they are introduced to various art techniques. Such words further reinforce their own judgment that they are not creative or artistic. If you say you cannot draw, it is because you have had that message reinforced to you ever since you were a child. You cannot draw representations of the external world, but you can draw thoughts and emotions. Our lives are what we create. If you think visually, your language and dreams create videos in your mind. It is useful to externalize those that are troubling us. Explore the blurred lines in our lives, in this case, between creativity, spirituality, and psychoeducation. At the center of it all stands the person, you and I. We contain and possibly are the creators and controllers of the energy.

Our bodies are systems of energy, and any movement we make is a movement of energy through a physical form. When our experience of the arts is mediated by a kinetic impulse, it touches us in a place that thinking cannot reach. The focus of many psychoeducational and therapeutic approaches is the cure or amelioration of what is wrong. This book is premised on the understanding that learning to deal well with that which is wrong is not a sufficient or sustainable condition for our well-being. Therefore, our organizational concern is to engage and develop the whole person. One systematic way of addressing the needs of the entire person is through the arts. As a source of relaxation and enrichment, the arts support a balanced and emotionally informed system.

3.1. Mind Mapping

A mind map is a highly organized visual expression of concepts, thoughts, and related information in relation to a particular topic or subject. It illustrates an array of critical thinking processes related to the central idea, which is usually (but not invariably) at the center of the mind map. This process can be spontaneous and allows for beyond-the-verbal representation. Mind mapping can also include the basic use of color-coding, rules, and lists, which can lead to remarkable improvements. According to Buzan, "In terms of presentations, these components can be added, deleted, or extended depending on the abilities needed to perceive the concept."

The visual language of mind mapping is extremely powerful. Research has shown that the use of both words and images, as opposed to using them separately, allows for two ways to remember information and create connections in order to understand its meaning. Tony says, "In having to think of an image, it requires that you absorb the information in a unique way for retention." Mind maps also allow for more conceptual means. As a system pitched for whole-brain thinking, mind maps help students conceptualize information in the same way in which the brain perceives information; therefore, clearly understanding memory and levels of comprehension.

3.2. Free Writing

Here's a suggested exercise to begin free writing. Spend fifteen minutes on each subject writing about each in turn. When the time period is up, put your pen down or stop typing, and immediately go on to the next subject. Above all, do not edit! Remember, also, it's okay to write down "I don't know what to write about" if you have nothing else to say about the prompt. Start. Even though free writing has the word "writing" in it, you don't actually have to write. Some people draw or doodle their free writes while others dictate to a tape recorder or use speech-to-text software. Pick what works for you. It's okay to speculate, to make wild word associations with things that enter your head or to completely jump the topic. No ideas are too big, too small, too crazy or too ordinary.

Usually done for a predetermined period of time, often ten minutes, the principle of free writing is that you simply write, allowing thoughts to flow without stopping to worry over spelling, punctuation, or thought development. The exercise is intended to loosen and free the mind and to encourage ideas, often revealing unexpected insight in mentally jammed areas. Free writing is also useful for those times when you have an active inner editor sitting on your shoulder longing to interject "As if!" or "What were you thinking?" It is an exercise intended to help you escape the tyranny of perfectionism and the overzealous inner critic.

3.3. Brainstorming

1. Quantity not Quality: The more quantity of ideas is produced, the better is the probability of getting a useful idea. 2. Freewheeling: Members can express themselves freely, without fear of criticism. 3. Combination of Ideas: Each one's ideas are shared and expressed openly. 4. No Evaluating: No suggestion is evaluated, only recorded.

No. 2: Brainstorming driving session: As soon as the problem is identified and clarified, start with a session of idea generation. Each member of the group will be asked for a feasible solution to the identified problem for which a group is created. It is usually facilitated by a leader who writes down the ideas generated in the session. Ideas are usually jotted down according to their relevance and commonality. The aim is to come up with the highest number of ideas possible in as short an amount of time as feasible. As an aid in idea generation, the psychiatrist Alex F. Osborn claims that fruitful aspects in brainstorming activity can be stimulated by the following 'Four Rules' of brainstorming:

No. 1: Problem Identification: The group identifies the problem that needs to be addressed. This could be related to specific technical details, parts of the product, or even the process used to develop the product. Ambiguities or confusion related to the problem are sorted during the identification phase by the group members.

To brainstorm, follow these two steps:

Brainstorming is the best-known, well-utilized, and universal idea generating technique. Many business professionals consider it as the most reliable technique for idea generation. This technique involves the generation of a large number of free-flying ideas on a given problem or situation. It is usually carried out in a group, where the inherent capability of an individual is released to generate a higher number of ideas.

3.4. Visualization

Visualization can be employed to furnish solutions to problems which would not necessarily lend themselves to solution by other, more formal, thought processes. The three-dimensional spatial questions and problems used to illustrate this variety of visualization can either be well known or they ought to be, for they are relatively fundamental. We all probably know a lot of them, certainly more than you will find here. If not, many simple books are available. The fact that they are well known and simple makes them ideal problem situations for the purpose of this exposition, as it enables us to concentrate on the introduction of the various visualization techniques involved and to overlook the intricacies of detailed complicated examples. Before we embark on these techniques, a dialectic about the utility and even the legitimacy of the process of visualization itself seems appropriate.

Before experiments are "done" in the mind or on paper, any seed of vision needs its proper soil of imagination in which it may cultivate itself. It may be possible to use one general principle for all domains of thinking! The mind must keep the possibility of something even beyond the space of all formal concepts. It imagines that this "something" can be seen and proceeds in its original direction. Contradiction cannot unsettle it since, strictly speaking, the mind is not aiming so much at statements that are true or false as it is as a model of some broader reality.

3.5. Collaborative Creativity

Combining all three levels of collaborations, the aspiring creative can accomplish in three sessions using four days the equivalent of what it takes three days to do with no peers and no Mavericks. These three iterative levels of conversation jump-start the creative process and bypass the desperately pernicious vacillation, contingency, and the dreaded self-sabotaging second-guessing that can occur morphing nascent original thoughts into mature, original, conceptually ground-breaking projects, whether they are artistic, scientific, or philosophical.

In addition to talking to counselors and mentors, like-minded peers should also be consulted. Many creative types side-step this essential stage of the creative process when they are working on a personal project that they neither want to give away nor be plagiarized. This is the very essence of the second iteration, about the idea not being ready and/or not ripe for public, or at least for social exposure: first iteration. Peers will inevitably have unique perspectives of where the project fits in with all extant projects and that tetrahedral querying freedom acts as a second iteration; they will recognize, prod and refine the fledgling differentials so that interesting, non-trivial category.

Skilled creative types can generate astounding results from the solitary mentoring environment. Nevertheless, in light of the recent rapid rise in global interconnectivity, it seems a shame not to cultivate circumstances in which the expertise of many may be brought to bear on a single individual. Consequently, as an alternative to one-on-one mentoring between the aspiring creative and the vastly world-wise, the aspiring creative can set up one-on-many teaching sessions. The aspiring creative should pick accomplished people from disparate backgrounds that are compatible with many of the different facets of her project. Homogeneity can lead to tastefully executed projects, but when it comes to gestating ineffable originality, the fertile ground of creativity grows in diversity and thrives with interspecific cross-pollination.

CHAPTER 4

Applying Creativity in Daily Life

Do you know how to let your creative intuition, or any type of intuitive or psychic knowledge in for that matter? Take a walk and clear your mind. Or work on a completely different project to allow yourself the freedom of movement and motion. Process, in some instances, acts as a sieve, autonomously employing the filtering process so that your artwork takes the form it is going to take. It is at this point in the process that the intuition of the artist and the different filters of processing become important. I have always been a practitioner of animism, of personification, for I believe we have to be in some frame of mind to obtain these results. We cannot, as Schiller states, dismember the muse. When an artist loses his/her connection to the divine within the creative process, this can prove disastrous. Only later, when the work is finished, can the artist truly spot these themes and fully understand the message encoded in the work itself.

Creativity can manifest in a variety of ways, including finding new uses for older items and problem solving. That is the kinetic part of creativity, the action-oriented process of making, inherently linking the artist to the art. But there is also a more passive type of manifesting that comes as a part of association, call it active meditation. In this creative process, the artist thinks of their art and forges links to why they act the way they do in their art and life. In other words, the artist actively associates life with their art. Every action in this artist's life is incubating the art for the next series or generation of work. Picasso states, "I paint the things I know to reveal the unknown."

www.ingramcontent.com/pod-product-compliance
Lightning Source LLC
Chambersburg PA
CBHW020736020526
44118CB00033B/1018